RECORDED VERSIONS GUITAR

**AUTHENTIC TRANSCRIPTIONS
WITH NOTES AND TABLATURE**

STONESOUR

Music transcriptions by Pete Billmann, Jeff Jacobson and Josh Rand

ISBN 0-634-05615-8

**HAL•LEONARD®
CORPORATION**

7777 W. BLUEMOUND RD. P.O. BOX 13819 MILWAUKEE, WI 53213

In Australia Contact:
Hal Leonard Australia Pty. Ltd.
22 Taunton Drive P.O. Box 5130
Cheltenham East, 3192 Victoria, Australia
Email: **ausadmin@halleonard.com**

Visit Hal Leonard Online at
www.halleonard.com

contents

Get Inside

Words and Music by Joel Ekman, Josh Rand and Shawn Economaki

Drop D tuning, down 1 1/2 steps:
(low to high) B-F#-B-E-G#-C#

Intro
Moderately fast ♩ = 154

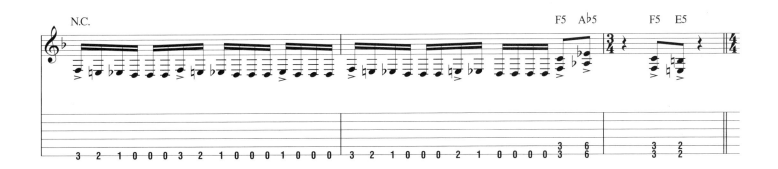

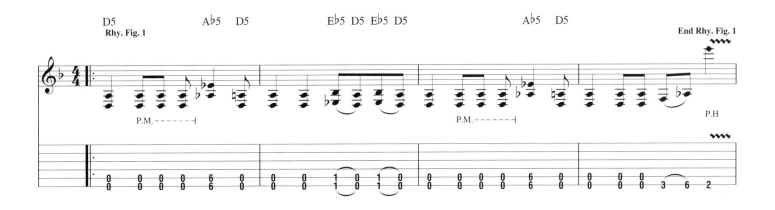

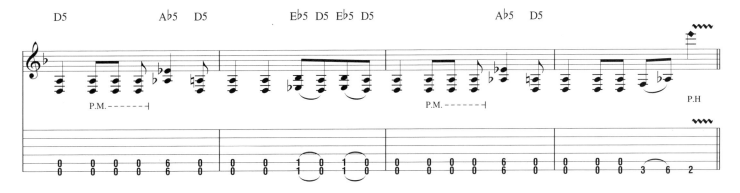

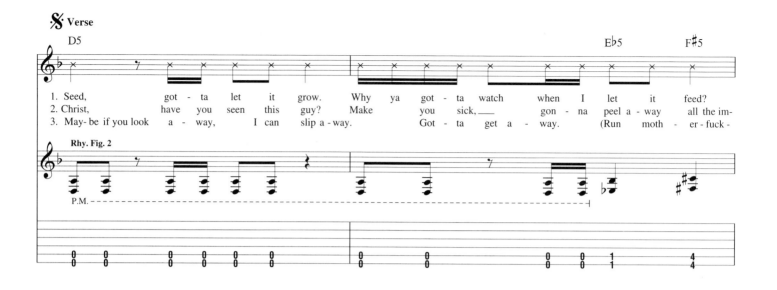

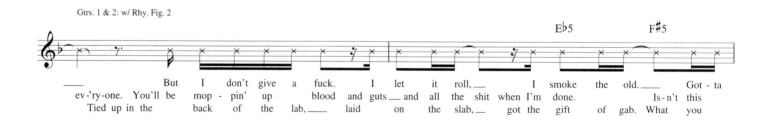

Half-time feel

Please wring the blood__ from my hands.__ Don't pre-tend__ that you un-

End half-time feel

-der-stand__ me. I don't e-ven want you__ look-in' at__ me.

(Moth-er-fuck-er, get in-side!__

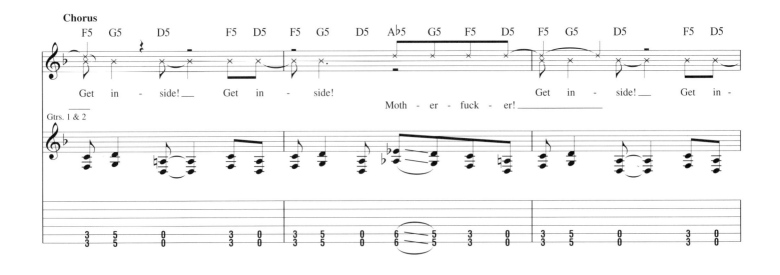

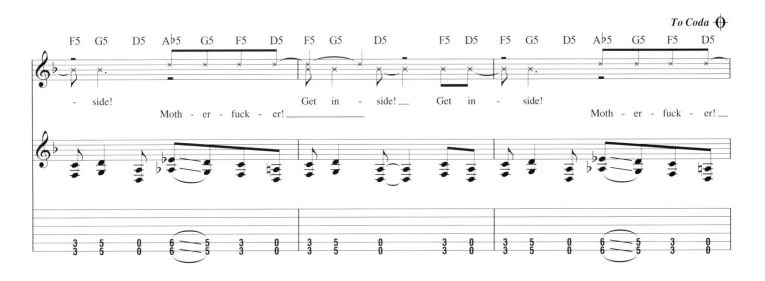

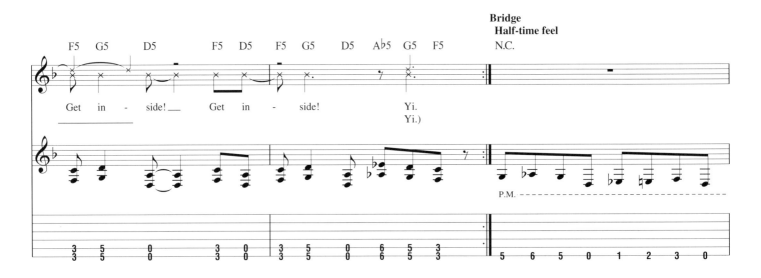

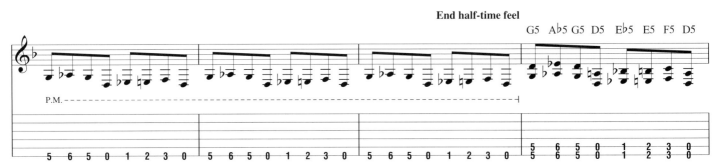

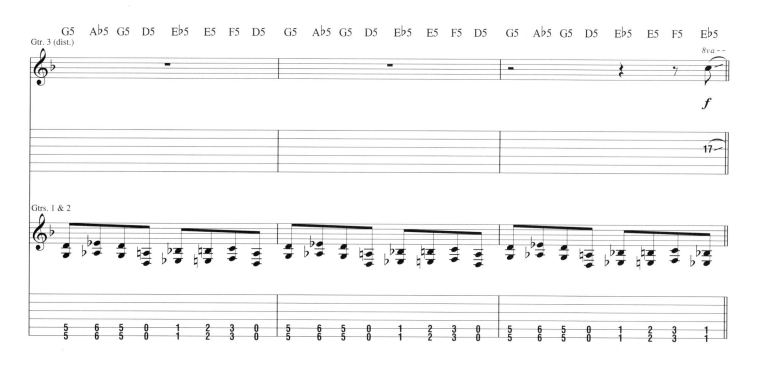

Guitar Solo

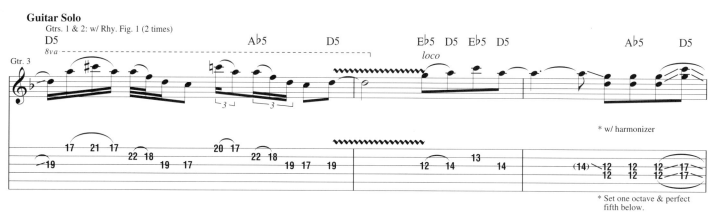

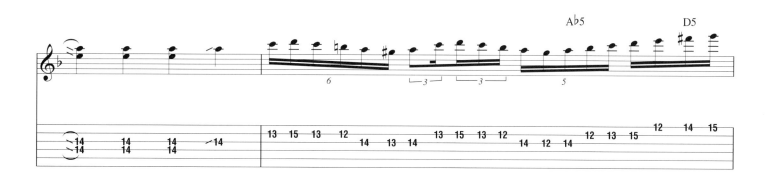

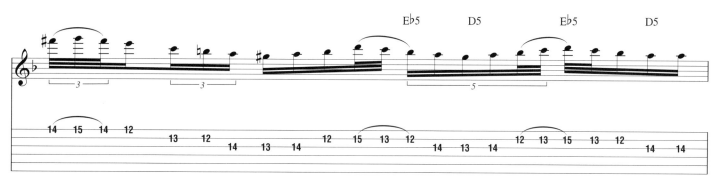

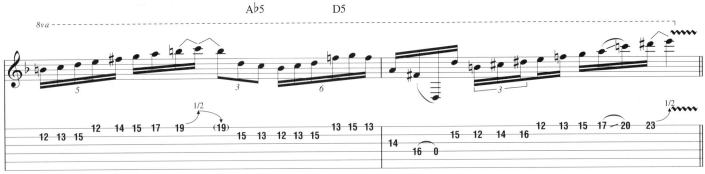

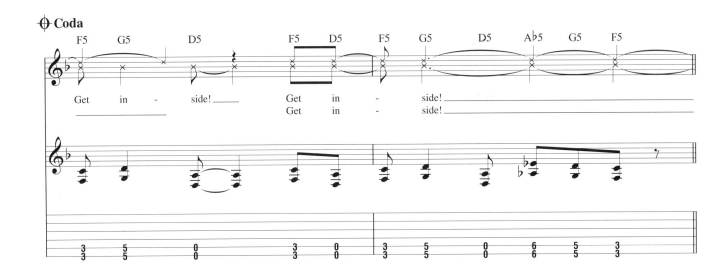

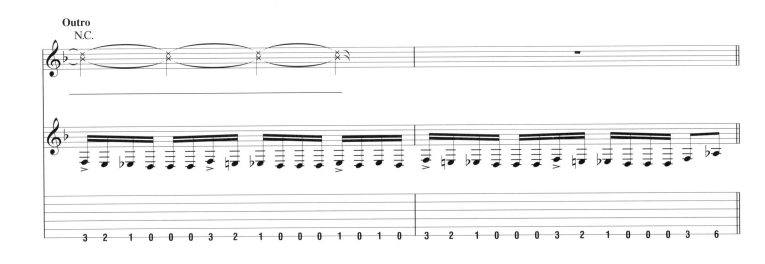

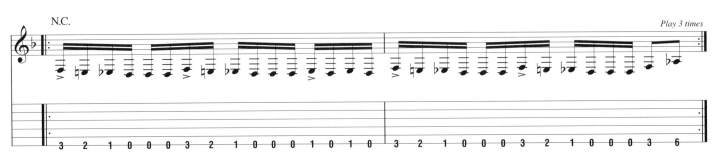

Orchids

Words and Music by Joel Ekman, Josh Rand and Shawn Economaki

Drop D tuning, down 1 1/2 steps:
(low to high) B-F#-B-E-G#-C#

Intro
Moderately ♩ = 112

* Gtr. 1
N.C.
Riff A

* Bass arr. for gtr.

Gtr. 1: w/ Riff A

D5

Yeah!

End Riff A   **Gtr. 2 (dist.)

†*pp*

**Doubled throughout   † Vol. swell

Rhy. Fig. 1   End Rhy. Fig. 1

f

Verse
Gtr. 2: w/ Rhy. Fig. 1 (2 times)
D5

1. You hold me___ in - side your i - ris like a, a ter - mi - nal stain___ on life.___
2. You keep me___ hid - den be - hind a cur - tain, an au - di - ble hu - man dis - play.
3. I live at___ arm's length and die a lit - tle be - tween your con - stants by ___ day.

You con - de - scend__ to my pri - mal brain and twist me 'round__ like a__ knife.__
You feed me__ or - chids to give me cour - age and keep me in line__ with dis - dain.
I want my___ soul back be - fore it's o - ver. I can't e - ven wish__ you a - way.

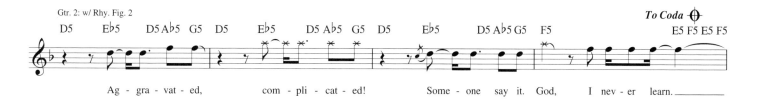

Gtr. 2: w/ Rhy. Fig. 2

To Coda ⊕

D5 E♭5 D5 A♭5 G5 D5 E♭5 D5 A♭5 G5 D5 E♭5 D5 A♭5 G5 F5 E5 F5 E5 F5

Ag - gra - vat - ed, com - pli - cat - ed! Some - one say it. God, I nev - er learn._____

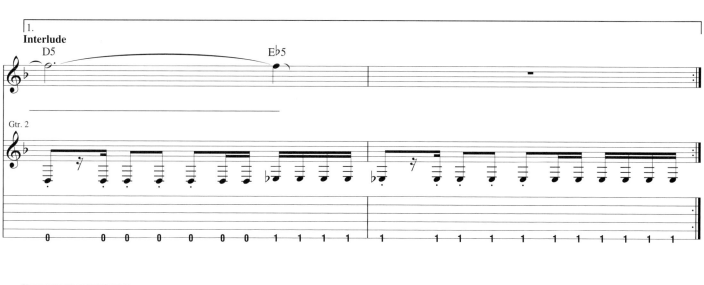

1.

Interlude

D5 E♭5

Gtr. 2

2.

Interlude

Gtr. 1: w/ Riff A (2 times)

D5

Gtr. 2

w/ flanger

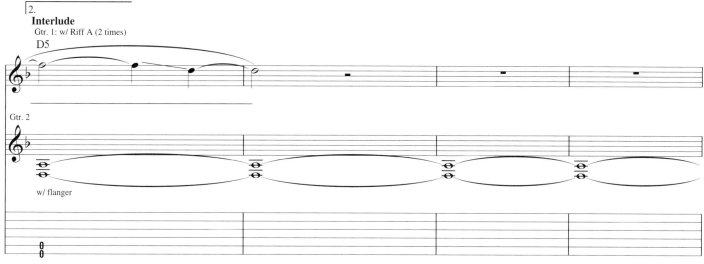

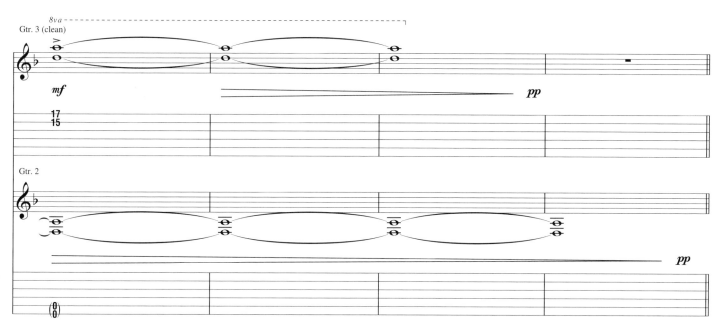

8va -

Gtr. 3 (clean)

mf   *pp*

Gtr. 2

pp

Cold Reader

Words and Music by Joel Ekman, Josh Rand and Shawn Economaki

* Chord symbols reflect implied harmony.

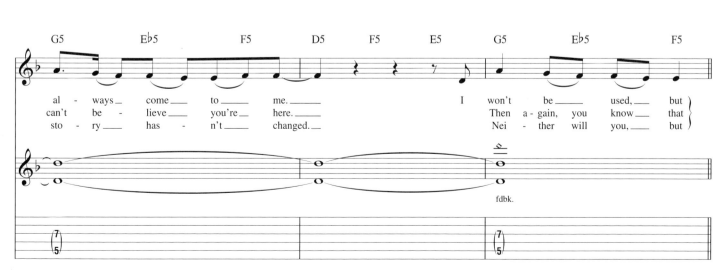

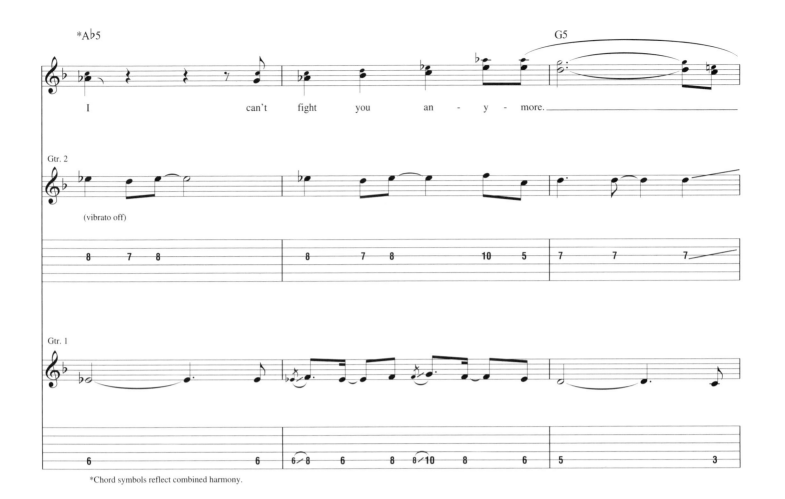

I can't fight you an-y-more.

(vibrato off)

*Chord symbols reflect combined harmony.

1. I know __ I'll o - pen up the door, __
2., 3. I know __ I'll o - pen up my soul, __

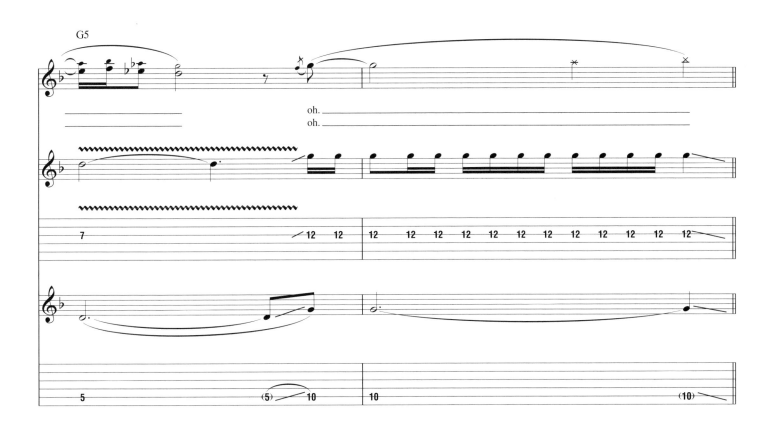

Chorus

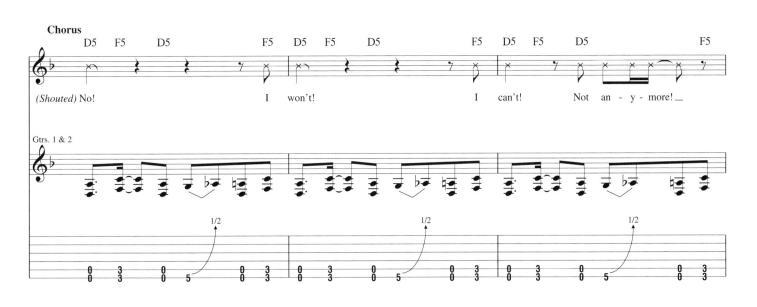

(Shouted) No!   I won't!   I can't!   Not an - y - more! __

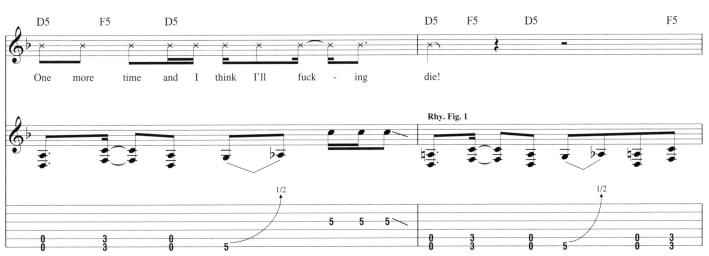

One more time and I think I'll fuck - ing die!

Blotter

Words and Music by Joel Ekman, Josh Rand and Shawn Economaki

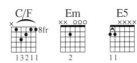

Drop D tuning, down 1 1/2 steps:
(low to high) B-F♯-B-E-G♯-C♯

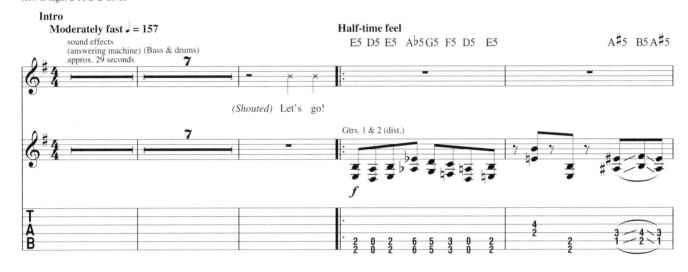

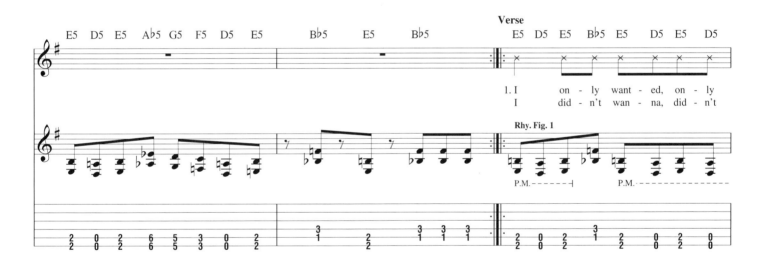

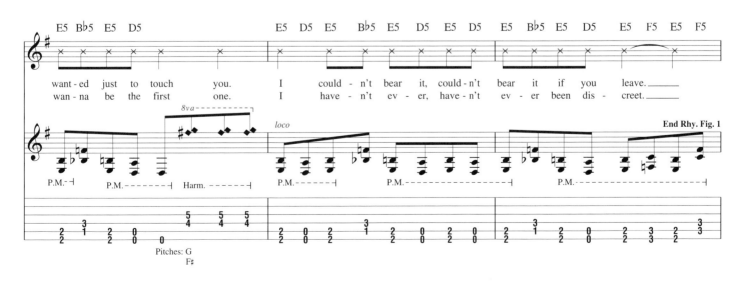

Interlude

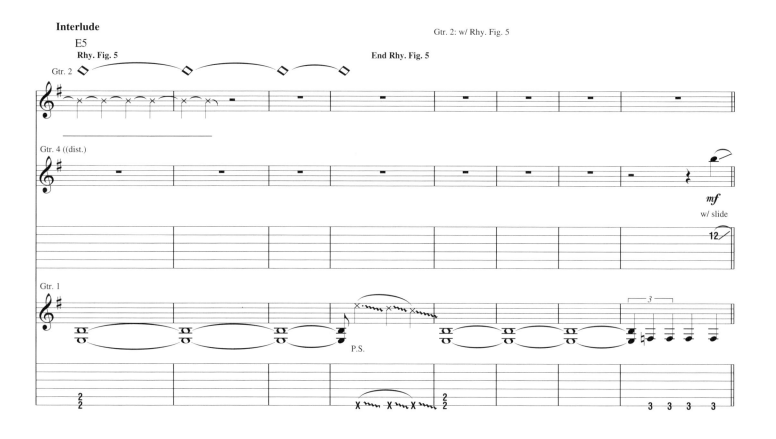

Bridge

Be-fore I show you where the se-cret is, I want to turn you in-to this.

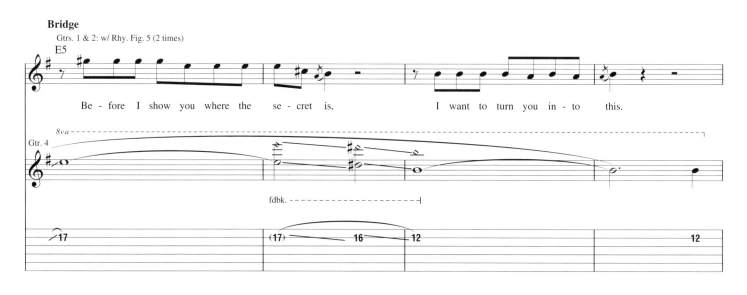

I want to give you all my noth-ing-ness, I want to cov-er you with this.

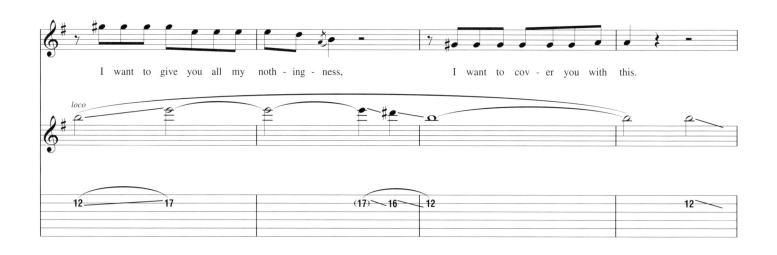

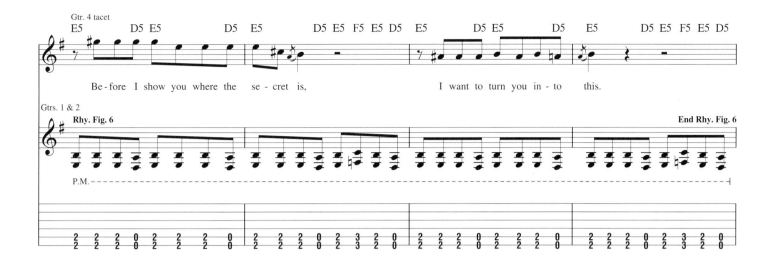

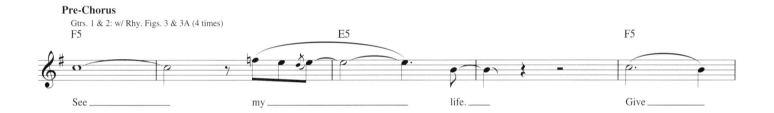

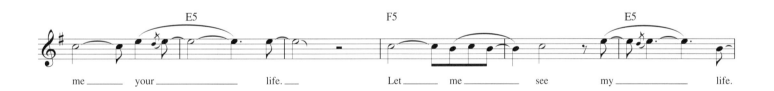

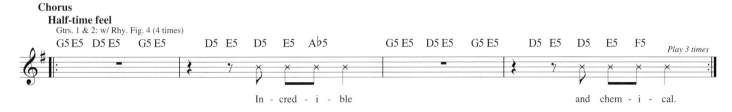

Choose

Words and Music by Joel Ekman, Josh Rand and Shawn Economaki

Drop D tuning, down 1 1/2 steps:
(low to high) B-F#-B-E-G#-C#

Intro
Moderately ♩ = 97

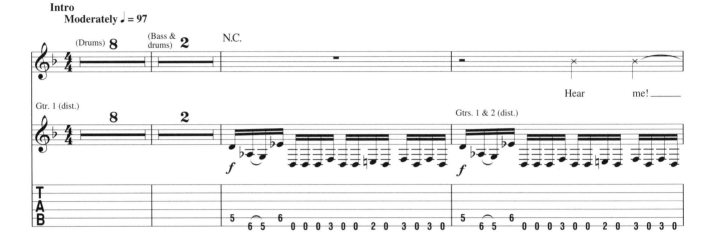

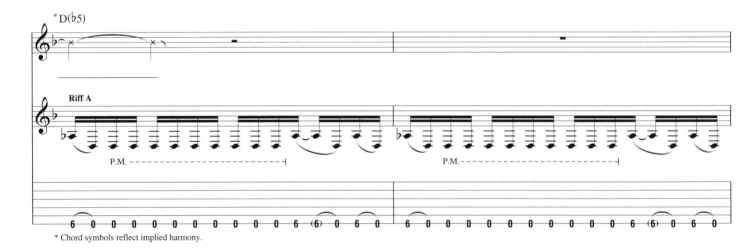

* Chord symbols reflect implied harmony.

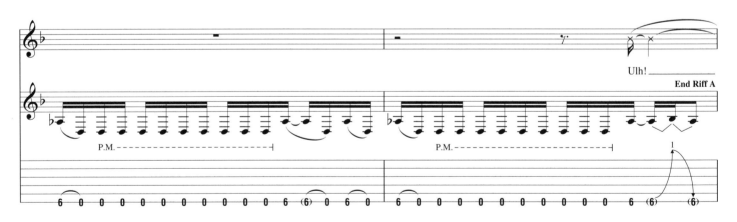

Verse

N.C.

1. Re-mem-ber all ___ the times ___ you bent our truth and crossed ___ our lines? ___ All things con-sid-ered, it was

just our nor-mal way ___ of life. ___ But some-where in the mid-dle, we got caught and dragged a-way. ___

Gtrs. 1 & 2

Fill 1   End Fill 1   Riff B

P.M. - - - - - - - - - - - - - - - -   P.M. - - - - - - - - - - - - - - - -

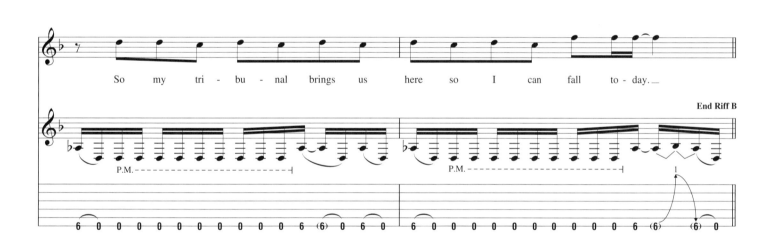

So my tri-bu-nal brings us here so I can fall to-day. ___

End Riff B

P.M. -   P.M. - - - - - - - - - - - - - - - -

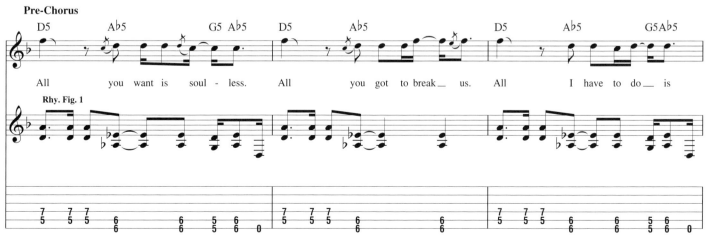

Pre-Chorus

D5   Ab5   G5 Ab5   D5   Ab5   D5   Ab5   G5 Ab5

All   you want is soul-less.   All   you got to break ___ us.   All   I have to do is

Rhy. Fig. 1

Monolith

Words and Music by Joel Ekman, Josh Rand and Shawn Economaki

Drop D tuning, down 1 1/2 steps:
(low to high) B-F#-B-E-G#-C#

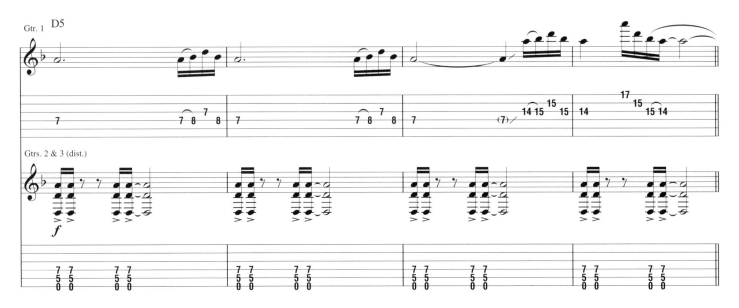

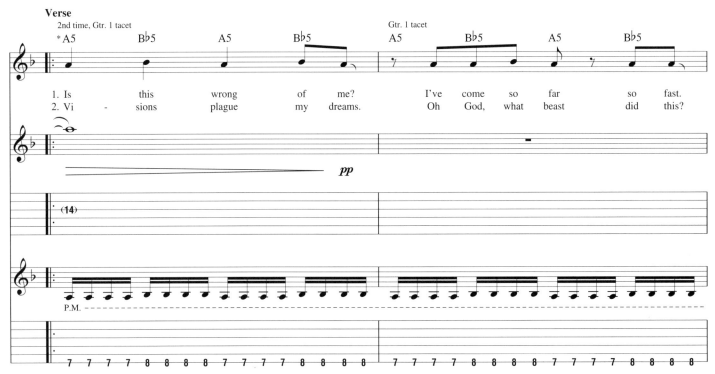

* Chord symbols reflect implied harmony.

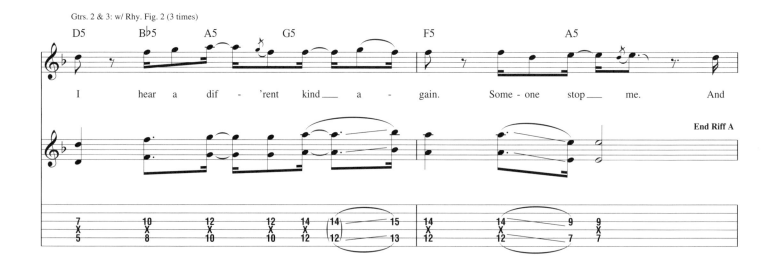

Gtrs. 2 & 3: w/ Rhy. Fig. 2 (3 times)

I hear a dif - 'rent kind_ a - gain. Some - one stop_ me. And

End Riff A

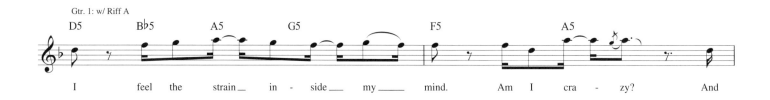

Gtr. 1: w/ Riff A

I feel the strain_ in - side_ my _ mind. Am I cra - zy? And

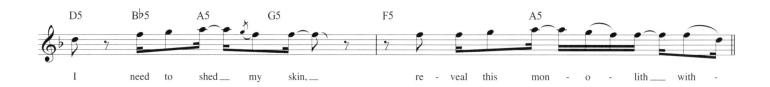

I need to shed_ my skin, _ re - veal this mon - o - lith_ with -

Interlude

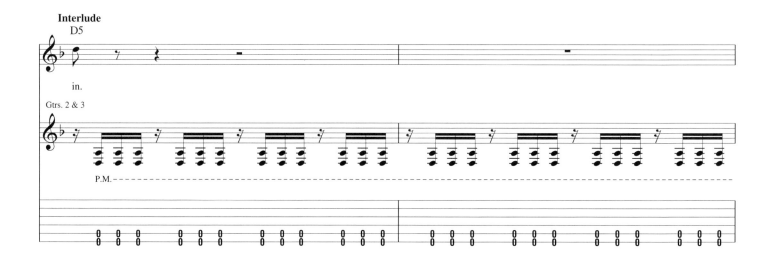

in.

Gtrs. 2 & 3

P.M.

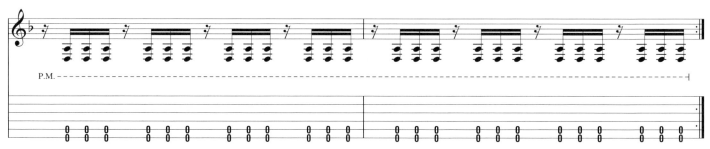

P.M.

Guitar Solo

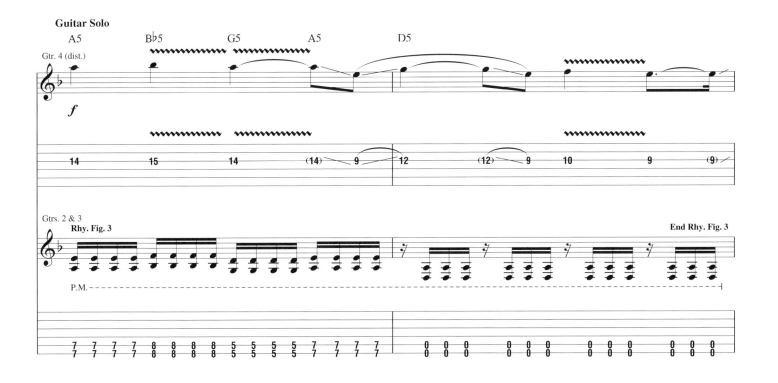

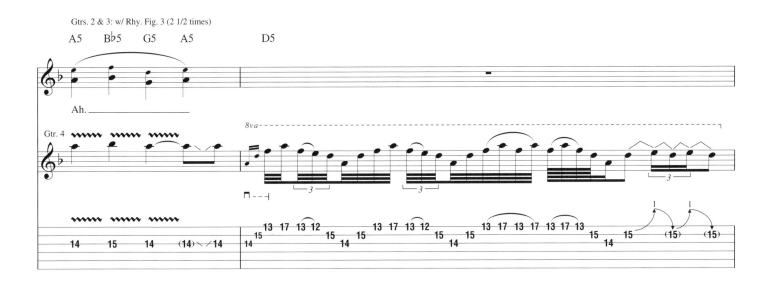

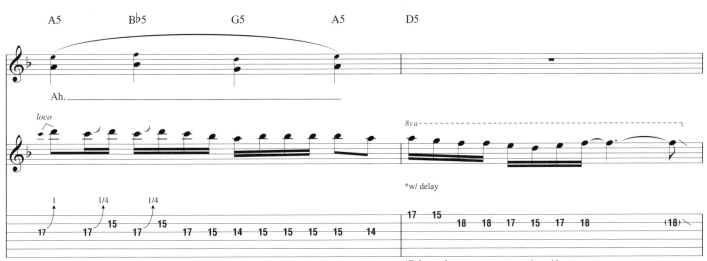

*Delay set for quarter note regeneration w/ 1 repeat.

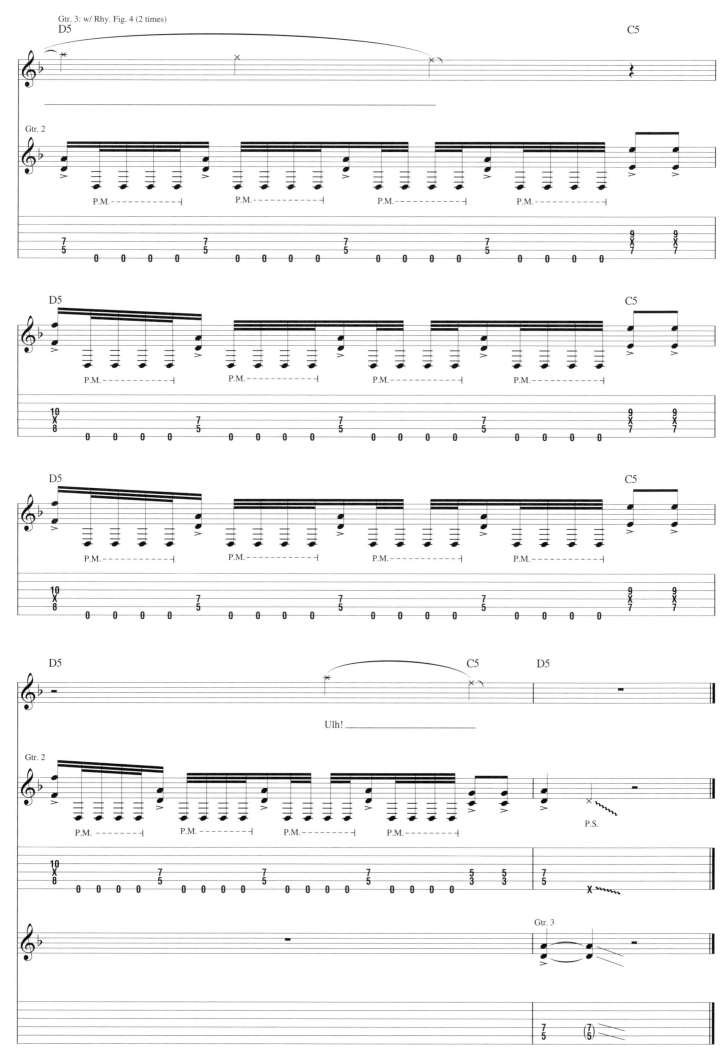

Inhale

Words and Music by Joel Ekman, Josh Rand and Shawn Economaki

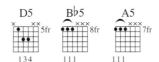

Drop D tuning, down 1 1/2 steps:
(low to high) B-F#-B-E-G#-C#

Intro

Moderately slow Rock ♩ = 100

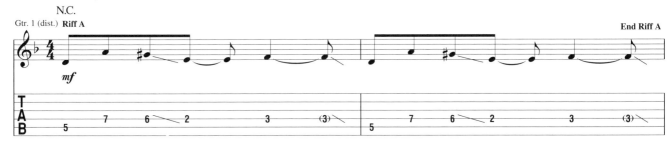

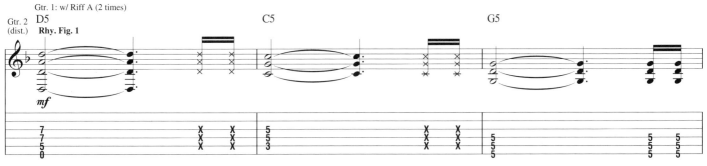

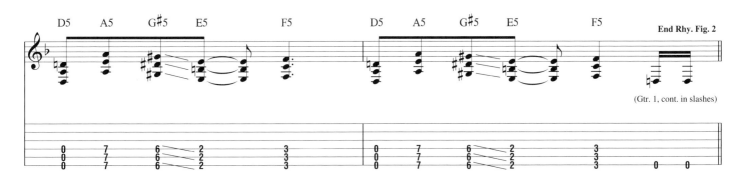

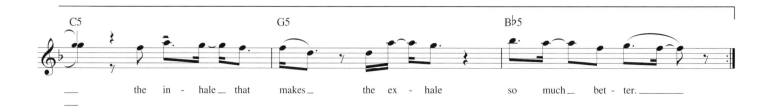

the in-hale___ that makes___ the ex-hale so much bet-ter._____

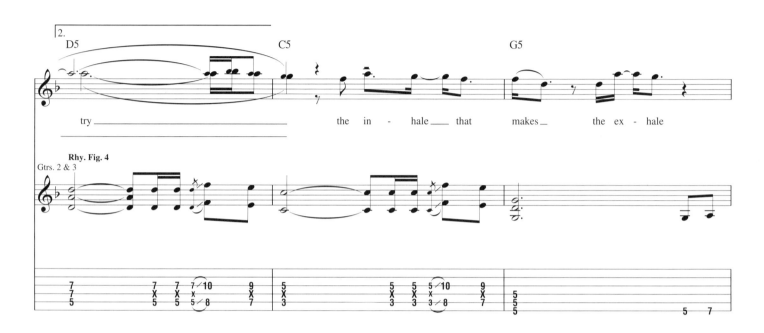

try_____ the in-hale___ that makes___ the ex-hale

Rhy. Fig. 4
Gtrs. 2 & 3

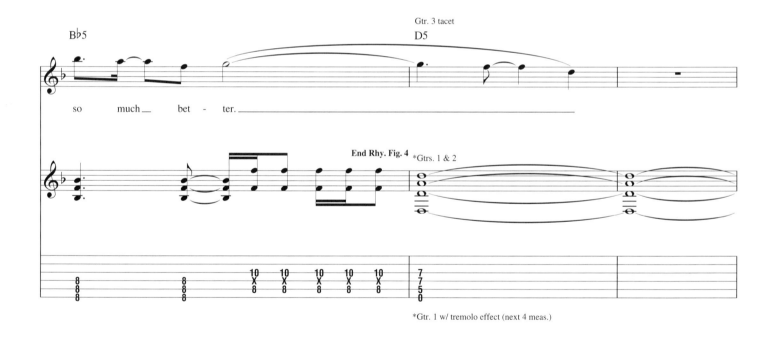

so much___ bet-ter._____

Gtr. 3 tacet

End Rhy. Fig. 4 *Gtrs. 1 & 2

*Gtr. 1 w/ tremolo effect (next 4 meas.)

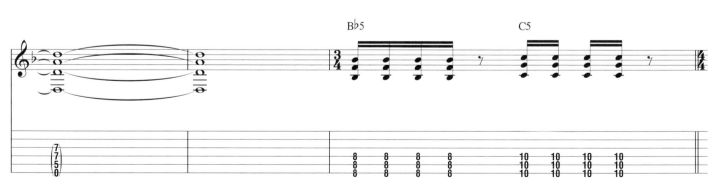

Bother

Words and Music by Corey Taylor

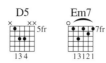

Tune down 1/2 step:
(low to high) E♭-A♭-D♭-G♭-B♭-E♭

Intro
Moderately slow ♩ = 96

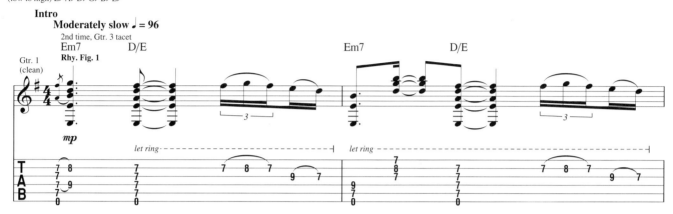

*2nd & 3rd times, Gtr. 1 tacet on beat 4.

Blue Study

Words and Music by Joel Ekman, Josh Rand and Shawn Economaki

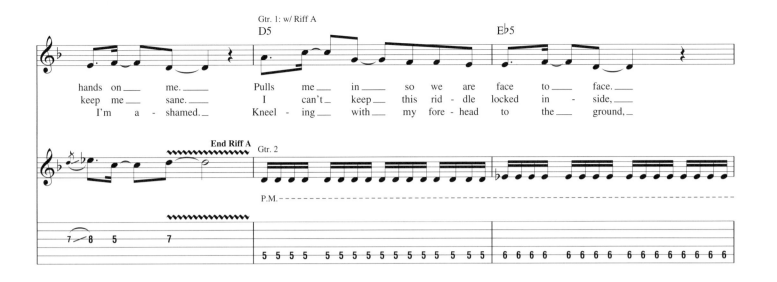

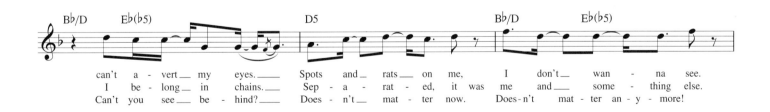

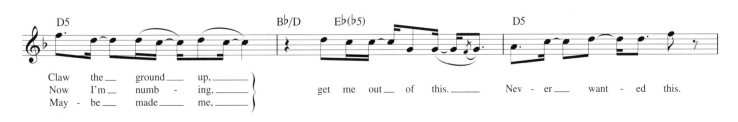

Guitar Solo

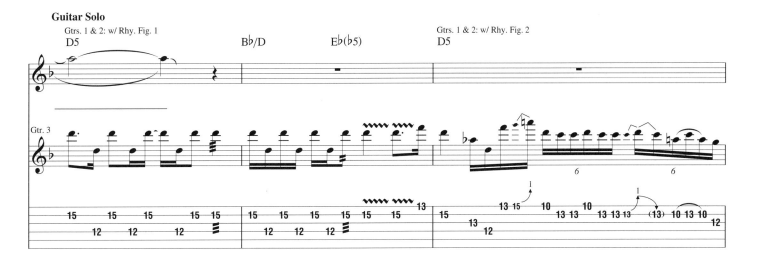

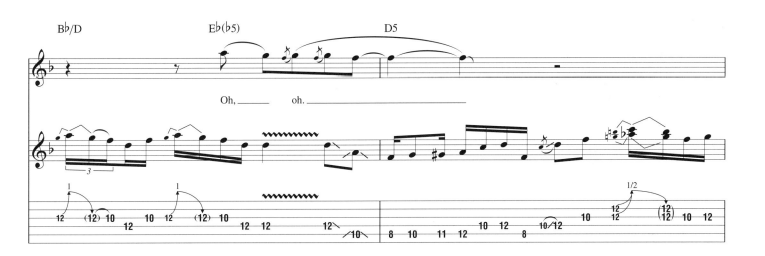

Oh, _____ oh. _____

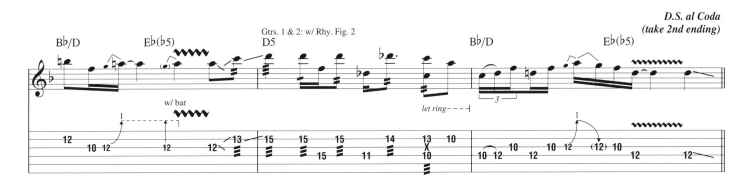

D.S. al Coda
(take 2nd ending)

And I left you, too.   Safe!   I just want to be   safe!

No!)

Take a Number

Words and Music by Joel Ekman, Josh Rand and Shawn Economaki

Gtrs. 1, 2 & 3: Drop D tuning, down 1/2 step:
(low to high) Db-Ab-Db-Gb-Bb-Eb
Gtr. 4: Double Drop D tuning, down 1/2 step:
(low to high) Db-Ab-Db-Gb-Bb-Db

Intro

Moderately slow Rock ♩ = 96

* Chord symbols reflect implied harmony.

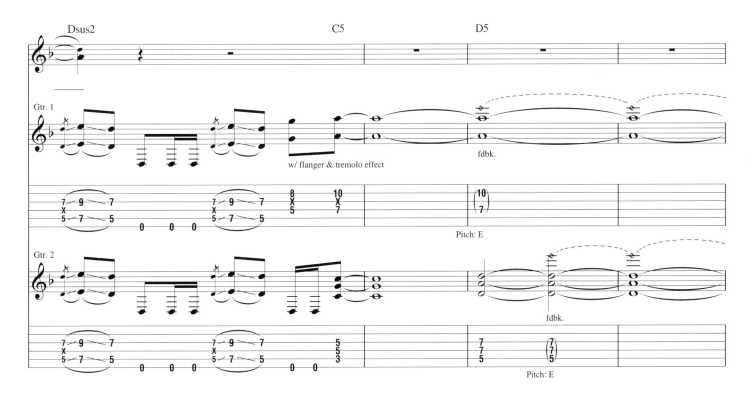

Verse

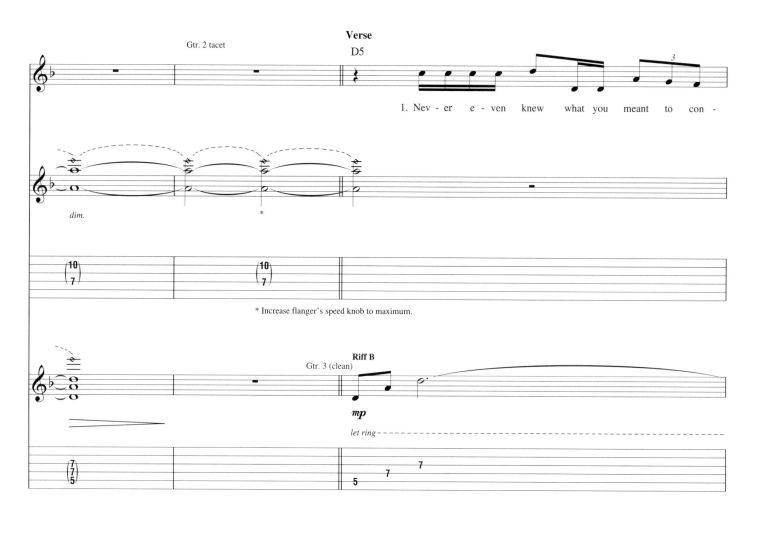

* Increase flanger's speed knob to maximum.

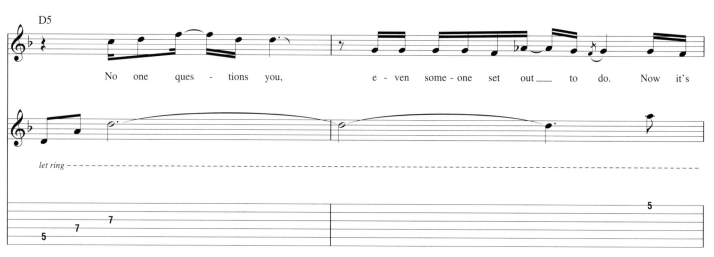

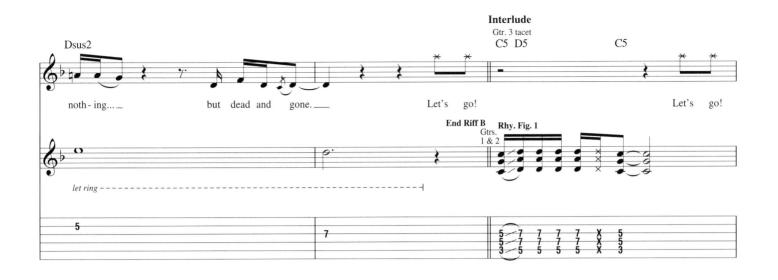

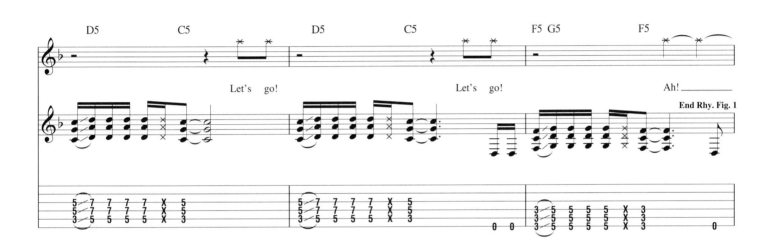

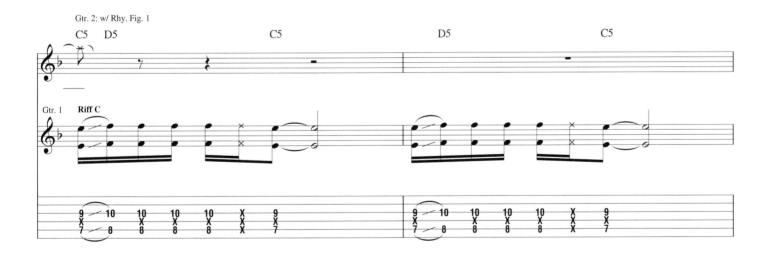

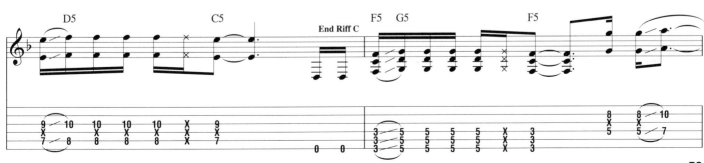

Bridge

Gtrs. 1 & 2: w/ Riff A (4 times)

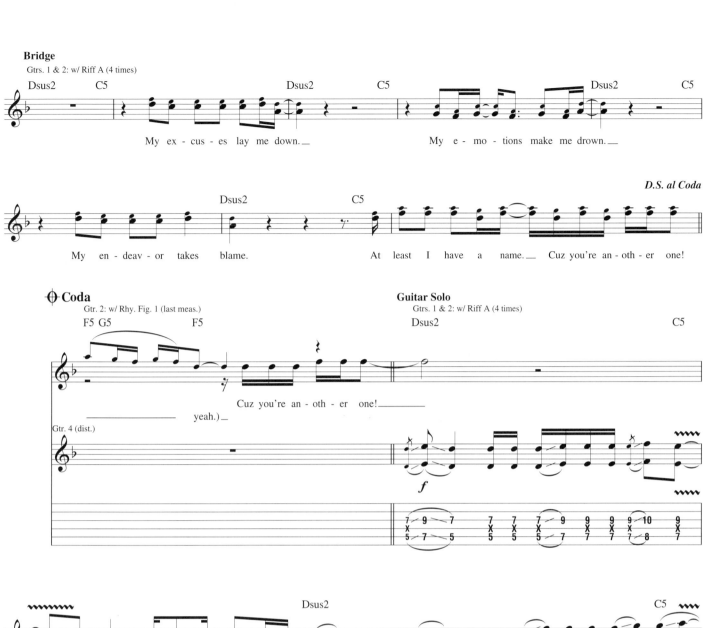

My ex - cus - es lay me down. ___

My e - mo - tions make me drown. ___

D.S. al Coda

My en - deav - or takes blame.

At least I have a name. ___ Cuz you're an - oth - er one!

Coda

Gtr. 2: w/ Rhy. Fig. 1 (last meas.)

Guitar Solo

Gtrs. 1 & 2: w/ Riff A (4 times)

Cuz you're an - oth - er one! ___

yeah.) ___

Gtr. 4 (dist.)

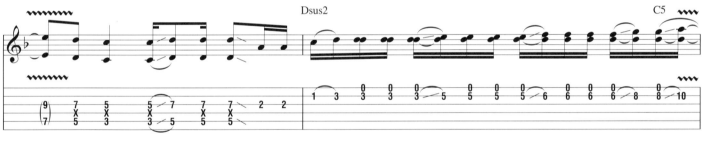

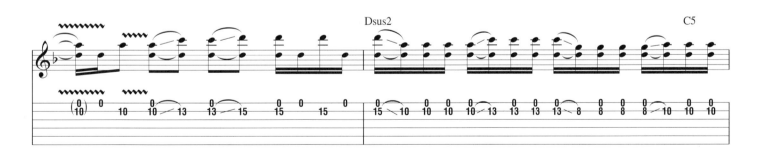

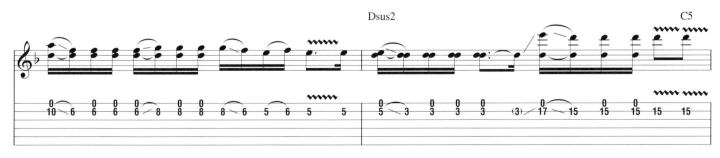

Outro
Gtrs. 1 & 2: w/ Riff A (3 times)

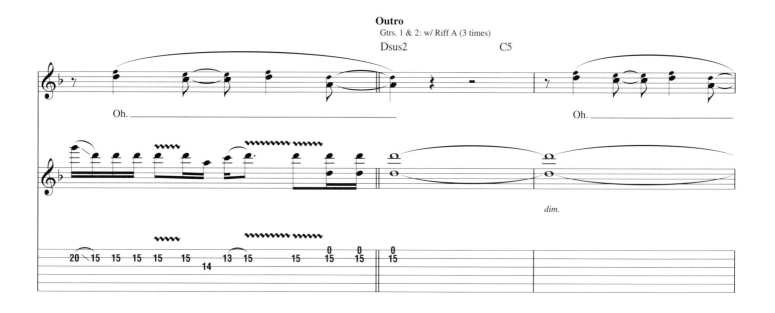

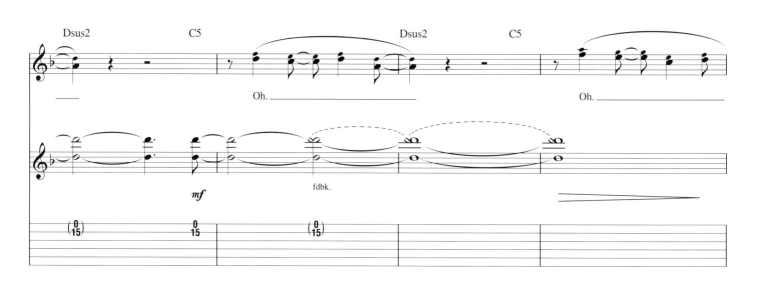

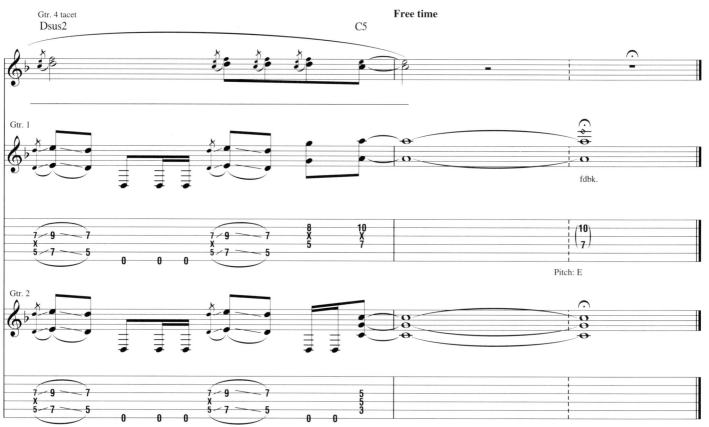

Idle Hands

Words and Music by Joel Ekman, Josh Rand and Shawn Economaki

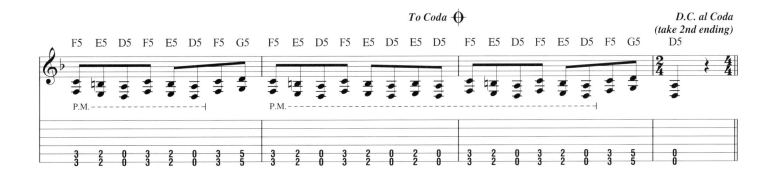

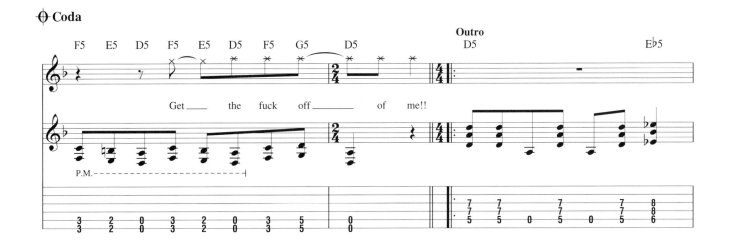

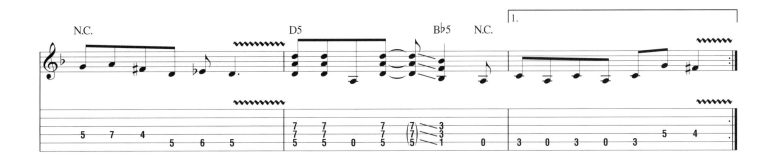

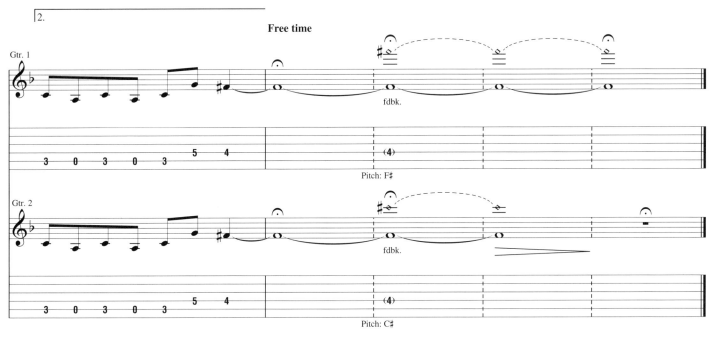

Tumult

Words and Music by Joel Ekman, Josh Rand and Shawn Economaki

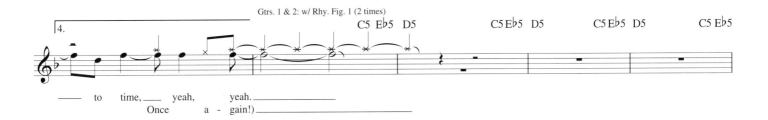

— to time,___ yeah,___ yeah._____
Once a - gain!)_____

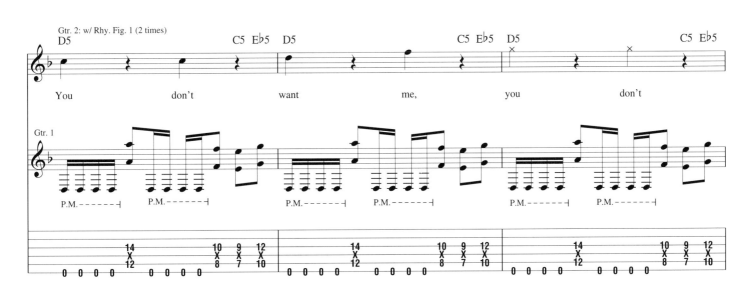

You don't want me, you don't

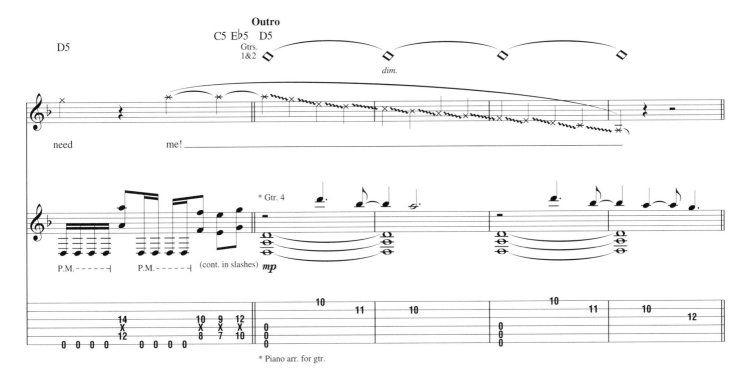

need me!_____

(cont. in slashes) *mp*

* Piano arr. for gtr.

Omega

By Joel Ekman, Josh Rand and Shawn Economaki

What a skeletal wreck of man this is
Translucent flesh and feeble bones
The kind of temple where the whores and villains try to tempt the holistic tones
Running rampant with free thought to free form in the free and clear
And the matters at hand are shelled out like lint at a laundromat
To sift and focus on the bigger, better, now
We all have a little sin that needs venting
Virtues for the rending
And laws and systems and stems of riff from the branches of office
Do you know what your post entails
Do you serve a purpose, or purposely serve
Wind down inside your atavistical lore
The value of a summer spent, and a winter earned
For the rest of us, there is always Sunday
The day of the week that reeks of rest
But all we do is catch our breath
So we can wade naked into the bloody pool
And place our hand on the Big Black Book
To watch the knives zigzag between our aching fingers
A vacation is a countdown
T minus your life and counting
Time to drag your tongue across the sugar cube and hope you get a taste
What the fuck is all this for
What the hell is goin' on
Shut up
I could go on and on
But, let's move on, shall we
Say, you're me and I'm you
And they all watch the things we do
And like a smack of spite, they threw me down the stairs
Haven't felt like this in years
The great magnet of malicious magnanimous refuse
Let me go and plunge me into the dead spot again
That's where you go when there's no one else around
It's just you
And there was never anyone to begin with, now was there
Sanctimonious pretentious dastardly bastards
With their thumb on the pulse and a finger on the trigger
Classified, my ass
That's a fucking secret and you know it
Government is another way to say
Better than you
It's like ice, but no pick
A murder charge that won't stick
It's like a whole other world where you can smell the food
But you can't touch the silverware
What luck
Fascism you can vote for
Isn't that sweet

And we're all gonna die someday
'Cause that's the American way
And I've drunk too much and said too little
When you're gaffer-taped in the middle
Say a prayer, save face
Get yourself together and
See what's happening
Shut up
Fuck you
Fuck you
I'm sorry, I could go on and on
But it's time to move on
So, remember, you're a wreck
An accident
Forget the freak, you're just nature
Keep the gun oiled and the temple clean
Shit, snort and blaspheme
Let the heads cool and the engine run
Because in the end, everything we do
Is just everything we've done

Guitar Notation Legend

Guitar Music can be notated three different ways: on a *musical staff*, in *tablature*, and in *rhythm slashes*.

RHYTHM SLASHES are written above the staff. Strum chords in the rhythm indicated. Use the chord diagrams found at the top of the first page of the transcription for the appropriate chord voicings. Round noteheads indicate single notes.

THE MUSICAL STAFF shows pitches and rhythms and is divided by bar lines into measures. Pitches are named after the first seven letters of the alphabet.

TABLATURE graphically represents the guitar fingerboard. Each horizontal line represents a a string, and each number represents a fret.

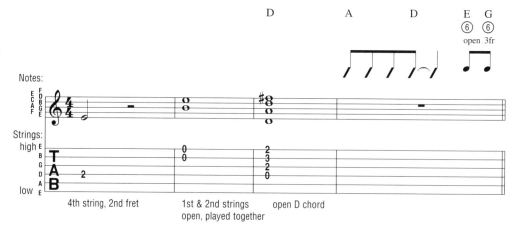

4th string, 2nd fret

1st & 2nd strings open, played together

open D chord

Definitions for Special Guitar Notation

HALF-STEP BEND: Strike the note and bend up 1/2 step.

WHOLE-STEP BEND: Strike the note and bend up one step.

GRACE NOTE BEND: Strike the note and immediately bend up as indicated.

SLIGHT (MICROTONE) BEND: Strike the note and bend up 1/4 step.

BEND AND RELEASE: Strike the note and bend up as indicated, then release back to the original note. Only the first note is struck.

PRE-BEND: Bend the note as indicated, then strike it.

PRE-BEND AND RELEASE: Bend the note as indicated. Strike it and release the bend back to the original note.

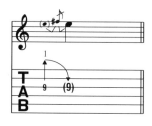

UNISON BEND: Strike the two notes simultaneously and bend the lower note up to the pitch of the higher.

VIBRATO: The string is vibrated by rapidly bending and releasing the note with the fretting hand.

WIDE VIBRATO: The pitch is varied to a greater degree by vibrating with the fretting hand.

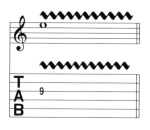

HAMMER-ON: Strike the first (lower) note with one finger, then sound the higher note (on the same string) with another finger by fretting it without picking.

PULL-OFF: Place both fingers on the notes to be sounded. Strike the first note and without picking, pull the finger off to sound the second (lower) note.

LEGATO SLIDE: Strike the first note and then slide the same fret-hand finger up or down to the second note. The second note is not struck.

SHIFT SLIDE: Same as legato slide, except the second note is struck.

TRILL: Very rapidly alternate between the notes indicated by continuously hammering on and pulling off.

TAPPING: Hammer ("tap") the fret indicated with the pick-hand index or middle finger and pull off to the note fretted by the fret hand.

NATURAL HARMONIC: Strike the note while the fret-hand lightly touches the string directly over the fret indicated.

PINCH HARMONIC: The note is fretted normally and a harmonic is produced by adding the edge of the thumb or the tip of the index finger of the pick hand to the normal pick attack.

HARP HARMONIC: The note is fretted normally and a harmonic is produced by gently resting the pick hand's index finger directly above the indicated fret (in parentheses) while the pick hand's thumb or pick assists by plucking the appropriate string.

PICK SCRAPE: The edge of the pick is rubbed down (or up) the string, producing a scratchy sound.

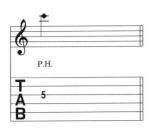

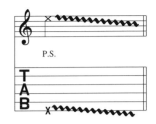

MUFFLED STRINGS: A percussive sound is produced by laying the fret hand across the string(s) without depressing, and striking them with the pick hand.

PALM MUTING: The note is partially muted by the pick hand lightly touching the string(s) just before the bridge.

RAKE: Drag the pick across the strings indicated with a single motion.

TREMOLO PICKING: The note is picked as rapidly and continuously as possible.

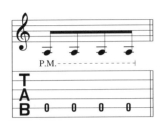

ARPEGGIATE: Play the notes of the chord indicated by quickly rolling them from bottom to top.

VIBRATO BAR DIVE AND RETURN: The pitch of the note or chord is dropped a specified number of steps (in rhythm) then returned to the original pitch.

VIBRATO BAR SCOOP: Depress the bar just before striking the note, then quickly release the bar.

VIBRATO BAR DIP: Strike the note and then immediately drop a specified number of steps, then release back to the original pitch.

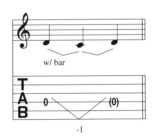

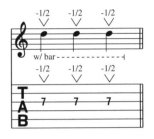

Additional Musical Definitions

(accent)	• Accentuate note (play it louder)	
(accent)	• Accentuate note with great intensity	
(staccato)	• Play the note short	
	• Downstroke	
V	• Upstroke	

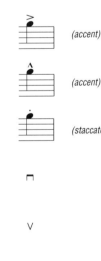

D.S. al Coda • Go back to the sign ($\%$), then play until the measure marked "*To Coda*," then skip to the section labelled "**Coda**."

D.C. al Fine • Go back to the beginning of the song and play until the measure marked "*Fine*" (end).

Rhy. Fig. • Label used to recall a recurring accompaniment pattern (usually chordal).

Riff • Label used to recall composed, melodic lines (usually single notes) which recur.

Fill • Label used to identify a brief melodic figure which is to be inserted into the arrangement.

Rhy. Fill • A chordal version of a Fill.

tacet • Instrument is silent (drops out).

• Repeat measures between signs.

1. 2. • When a repeated section has different endings, play the first ending only the first time and the second ending only the second time.

NOTE: Tablature numbers in parentheses mean:
1. The note is being sustained over a system (note in standard notation is tied), or
2. The note is sustained, but a new articulation (such as a hammer-on, pull-off, slide or vibrato begins), or
3. The note is a barely audible "ghost" note (note in standard notation is also in parentheses).

RECORDED VERSIONS
The Best Note-For-Note Transcriptions Available

ALL BOOKS INCLUDE TABLATURE